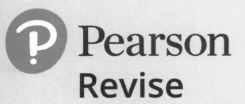

Pearson
Revise

Catch-Up 2020 Revision pack

Pearson Edexcel GCSE (9–1)
English Language

Includes
Knowledge check diagnostic self-test
Revision Guide
and
Revision Workbook

Knowledge check

REVISE EDEXCEL GCSE (9–1)
English Language
REVISION GUIDE
for the 9–1 exams

REVISE EDEXCEL GCSE (9–1)
English Language
REVISION WORKBOOK
for the 9–1 exams

Pearson

Get back on track

The COVID-19 pandemic has been disruptive for students of all ages around the world. And if you're preparing for your GCSEs then it's especially important that you catch up on any work you've missed. This pack is designed to help you revise and practise any topics you might need a reminder on, and stay on track for success in your Pearson Edexcel English Language GCSE course.

Time for a check-up

Take the **Knowledge check** diagnostic self-test to help you identify which topics and skills you need to recap. The questions in this test focus on key skills and core knowledge that you will need to know to succeed in the rest of your GCSE course, and in your exams.

You can mark your own work using the **answers** on pages 18 and 19 of this booklet. If you struggle with any of the questions, just add the Revision Guide page numbers for that question to your custom catch-up plan on page 14. Then you can revise and practise that topic and build your confidence.

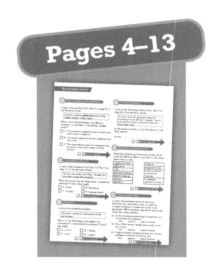

Pages 4–13

Make a plan

Create your own custom **Catch-up plan** by entering the page numbers you need to revise in this table. You can use the tick boxes to track your progress, and there is space to add any extra notes from your teacher or tutor.

Pages 14–15

Stress-free studying

Here are a few top tips from our experts to stay healthy and sane when things get busy!

- Set yourself simple targets, like reviewing a couple of pages of the Revision Guide in a 20-minute study session.
- Phone a friend! If you're struggling with a topic, ask one of your friends if they've figured it out and can explain it to you.
- Find a quiet space at home or at school – use headphones if it helps you to concentrate.
- Put your phone on silent, and try not to get distracted by TV or the internet.
- Drink plenty of water, get plenty of sleep, take breaks and stay active!

Once you have identified your target topics and created your catch-up plan, it's time to break open the books and get revising. The Revision Guide and Revision Workbook in your pack have matching page numbers to help you find your way around quickly and easily.

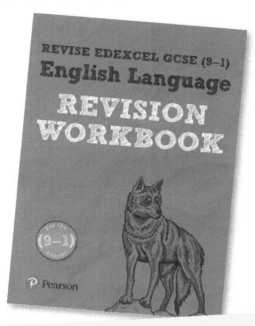

Your **Revision Guide** is packed with essential facts, key skills and worked examples to help you stay ahead of the game. Each page covers a single topic so you can stay organised, and the book covers your **whole course**, so once you're back up to speed you will be able to use it alongside your school work, and to revise for your exams.

Check that you have nailed each topic by practising some exam-style questions on the corresponding page in the **Revision Workbook**. There are **guided questions** which give you part of the working, and hints and tips to help you get started. And when the exams are a bit closer, you can use the **exam-style practice papers** to check that you are exam-ready.

Find your catch-up topics

If you know which topics you want to revise, you can use the **Matching chart** to find the corresponding Revision Guide and Workbook pages. Your teacher or tutor might be able to tell you which topics you missed, or you might recognise them from the work you did at home during lockdown.

Tick the units or topics you want to revise, then add those page numbers to your catch-up plan on page 14.

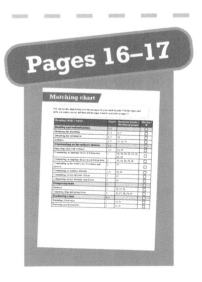

Pages 16–17

Knowledge check

You can use the diagnostic self-test on the next 10 pages to help you create your own customised catch-up plan. Each question checks a different key skill or piece of core knowledge from your GCSE course. If you feel that you need more help with that topic or skill, add the page numbers shown in the arrows to your catch-up plan. You can mark your work using the answers on pages 18 and 19 of this booklet.

Texts in the Revision Guide

You will need to read short extracts of texts to answer some of the questions in this quiz. You can find these texts in the Revision Guide included with this pack. You will be told in the question if you need to read an extract, and you will be given a page reference in the Revision Guide.

Reading

1 Key features of texts

You will read one fiction and two non-fiction texts in your exam. Draw lines linking each text type with the key features you need to think about as you read them.

In a **fiction** text you need to think about
In a **non-fiction** text you need to think about

purpose
character
atmosphere
tone
point of view

☑ ☒ Revise page 2

2 Questions and key words

Look at this exam-style question:

> In lines 5–14, how does the writer use language and structure to show Elizabeth's fear? Support your views with reference to the text.
> **(6 marks)**

Which of the following phrases are key pieces of information in the question that will help you write your answer? Tick all that apply.

☐ **A** lines 5–14   ☐ **B** language and structure

☐ **C** Elizabeth's fear   ☐ **D** reference to the text

☑ ☒ Revise pages 3, 4, 5

3 Skim reading

Which one of the following is an effective method of **skim reading**?

☐ **A** Reading very quickly.

☐ **B** Reading every other word.

☐ **C** Reading the heading, the first sentence of each paragraph and the final sentence of the text.

☐ **D** Focusing on just the shorter words in a text.

☑ ☒ Revise pages 6, 7

4 Identifying key information

Look at the extract from *The Half-Brothers* on page 10 of the Revision Guide. What is stopping the narrator from finding his way home? Tick one box.

☐ **A** It has been snowing.

☐ **B** It is dark.

☐ **C** He does not know the way.

☐ **D** He is too tired to walk.

☑ ☒ Revise page 10

5 **Reading between the lines**

Look at lines 1–10 of the extract from *The Adventures of Tom Sawyer* on page 98 of the Revision Guide. Write down the **first** word that suggests Becky and Tom are children.

Answer: ....

☑ ☒ **Revise pages 11, 12**

6 **Decoding unfamiliar words**

Look at lines 1–3 of Text 6 on page 101 of the Revision Guide. The word "virago" means aggressive woman. Which one of the following words in the sentences around this word does **not** provide a clue to help you guess its meaning?

☐ **A** facing   ☐ **B** screaming

☐ **C** sullen   ☐ **D** stranger

☑ ☒ **Revise page 13**

7 **Quotation punctuation**

Look at this student's analysis of lines 1–12 from Text 2 on page 97 of the Revision Guide. Circle **three** different punctuation errors in the student's work.

> The narrator makes us feel sorry for him. He tells us he was "doubly an orphan because both his parents are dead, and that he had been "reared in a workhouse" and, even though he works hard, he is not respected in his job I, Samuel Lowgood, who had worked and slaved and drudged, had been snubbed, throughout eleven long weary years".

☑ ☒ **Revise page 14**

8 **Point, evidence, explain**

Look again at the student's work in question 7. Which one of the following is missing from the student's analysis?

☐ **A** a point

☐ **B** evidence to support the point

☐ **C** an explanation of how the evidence supports the point

☑ ☒ **Revise page 15**

9 **Noun, adjective, verb, adverb**

Look at this student's comment on the writer's language choice in Text 2 on page 97 of the Revision Guide:

> The adjectives "worked", "slaved" and "drudged" emphasise how hard and difficult the narrator found his job.

What mistake has this student made in their comment?

Answer: ....

....

☑ ☒ **Revise page 18**

10 **Connotations**

Look at this sentence from Text 10 on page 105 of the Revision Guide:

> It's cold, it's dark and you've got to **bolt** your breakfast before dragging a bag full of papers round the streets.

Which of the following are the connotations of the verb "bolt"? Tick all that apply.

☐ **A** speed   ☐ **B** panic

☐ **C** tasteless   ☐ **D** unenjoyable

☑ ☒ **Revise page 19**

Knowledge check

11 Simile, metaphor and personification

Look at this sentence from Text 4 on page 99 of the Revision Guide:

> Only the noiseless, **pitiless snow** kept falling thicker, thicker—faster, faster!

Which one of the following is an effective comment on the effect of the phrase "pitiless snow"?

☐ **A** This metaphor suggests the snow is heavy and thick which is dangerous.

☐ **B** This simile implies the weather is getting worse and worse.

☐ **C** This personification gives the impression that the snow is cruel and is trying to kill the narrator.

☑ ☒ **Revise page 20**

12 Commenting on character

Look at these sentences from line 6 of Text 5 on page 100 of the Revision Guide:

> The thin one cackles, Oh, God, I thought you were here to clean the lavatories.

What techniques has the writer used to create this character? Tick all that apply.

☐ **A** action   ☐ **B** description

☐ **C** dialogue   ☐ **D** language choice

☑ ☒ **Revise page 21**

13 Atmosphere

Look at this student's comment:

> The writer creates an atmosphere of fear and tension.

Which of the following could replace "an atmosphere" in this student's comment? Tick all that apply.

☐ **A** a mood   ☐ **B** a feeling

☐ **C** a tone   ☐ **D** a register

☑ ☒ **Revise page 22**

14 First and third person

Look at the following sentence from Text 4 on page 99 of the Revision Guide:

> It looked dark and gloomy enough; but everything was so still that I thought I should have plenty of time to get home before the snow came down.

Is this sentence written in the first person or the third person?

Answer: ....

☑ ☒ **Revise page 23**

15 The effects of rhetorical devices

Draw lines linking each rhetorical device below to all the different effects it can have on the reader when used in a text.

a pattern of three	emphasis
alliteration	engage the reader
a list	create an extreme or emotional response
rhetorical question	
emotive language	
contrast	to highlight quantity or variety
repetition	

☑ ☒ **Revise pages 25, 26**

16 Adding persuasiveness

Look at the sentences below. In each one, the writer has used either a fact, an opinion, or expert evidence to make their point more persuasive. Which sentence uses which technique? Circle the correct answers.

(a) In the last century, technology has improved our lives beyond all recognition.

   fact   opinion   expert evidence

(b) Over 40% of human beings cannot easily access the internet.

   fact   opinion   expert evidence

(c) Professor Stephen Hawking warned that artificial intelligence could end the human race.

   fact   opinion   expert evidence

☑ ☒ **Revise page 27**

17 Sentence structure

Look at one student's comment on a sentence from Text 10 on page 105 of the Revision Guide.

> "It's cold, it's dark and you've got to bolt your breakfast before dragging a bag full of papers round the streets." The writer uses this long single-clause sentence to highlight how early you have to get up to do a paper round.

What two errors has this student made in their comment on the writer's use of sentence structure?

Answer 1: ....

....

2: ....

....

☑ ☒ **Revise pages 28, 29**

18 Text structure

Both fiction and non-fiction texts can be structured with an opening or introduction, a development, and a conclusion or ending. Draw lines linking each structural feature to the job it does.

| Introduction or opening |
| Development |
| Ending or conclusion |

| Leaves the reader with a lasting impression |
| Sets the scene |
| Holds the reader's interest to keep them reading |

☑ ☒ **Revise pages 30, 31**

19 Synthesis

Text 9 on page 104 of the Revision Guide is about the writer's experience of becoming a taxi driver and Text 10 on page 105 explores why young people are no longer prepared to do a paper round. Which two pieces of evidence best support the following point?

> Both writers focus on the challenges and difficulties of the job.

Text 9: tick one box

☐ **A** I started learning the Knowledge of London in October 2008

☐ **B** out on their moped come rain, freezing wind, or traffic chaos

☐ **C** the examiners would play games such as putting the chair in the examination room facing the wrong direction

Text 10: tick one box

☐ **D** It's cold, it's dark and you've got to bolt your breakfast before dragging a bag full of papers round the streets.

☐ **E** a lot of newsagents have given up trying to find kids to do it

☐ **F** I'd have to deliver the papers myself to stop customers getting angry

☑ ☒ **Revise pages 34, 35, 36**

20 Comparing two points of view

Look at the first paragraphs of Text 7 on page 102 and Text 8 on page 103 of the Revision Guide. Which of the statements below do you agree with? Tick all that apply.

☐ **A** Both writers are positive about their experience.

☐ **B** Both writers are negative about their experience.

☐ **C** Both writers choose language with negative connotations.

☐ **D** Both writers use contrast to highlight their views.

☑ ☒ **Revise pages 37, 38, 39, 40**

Knowledge check

21 Evaluation

Which of the statements will complete the sentence to make a true statement?
Tick all that apply.

When you evaluate a text, you need to:

- [ ] **A** support your ideas with evidence or reference to the text.
- [ ] **B** clearly state how much you enjoyed reading it and why.
- [ ] **C** analyse language and structure in detail.
- [ ] **D** comment on how well the writer has achieved what they set out to do.

☑ ☒ Revise pages 42, 43, 44 ➤

Writing

22 Imaginative writing

Which one of the following techniques would you be **least likely** to use when you write an imaginative text? Tick all that apply.

- [ ] **A** the five senses
- [ ] **B** figurative language
- [ ] **C** first person
- [ ] **D** facts and statistics

☑ ☒ Revise page 50 ➤

23 Writing to inform, explain or review

Which one of the following techniques would you be **least likely** to use when you write to inform, explain or review?

- [ ] **A** headings and subheadings
- [ ] **B** formal tone
- [ ] **C** rhetorical devices
- [ ] **D** facts and statistics

☑ ☒ Revise page 51 ➤

24 Writing to argue or persuade

Which one of the of the following techniques would you be **least likely** to use when you write to argue or persuade?

- [ ] **A** evidence
- [ ] **B** figurative language
- [ ] **C** counter arguments
- [ ] **D** facts and statistics

☑ ☒ Revise page 52 ➤

25 Register and audience

In which one of these writing texts are you **most likely** to use some informal language?

- [ ] **A** A letter to your local council.
- [ ] **B** A speech to a Year 11 assembly.
- [ ] **C** An information leaflet about a local sporting event.
- [ ] **D** A newspaper article in which you give your views on a controversial subject.

☑ ☒ Revise page 53 ➤

26 Form

Look at the three text forms below. Which of the following features would you be **most likely** to use in each of these text forms? Circle all that apply.

(a) A letter

your address   sub-heading   bullet points

(b) A newspaper article

your address   sub-heading   bullet points

(c) An information guide

your address   sub-heading   bullet points

☑ ☒ **Revise page 56, 57, 58** ➤

27 Planning imaginative writing

A short story can be structured in these five parts. Write numbers 1–5 to show the order in which they are usually sequenced.

.... falling action

.... resolution

.... rising action

.... exposition

.... climax

☑ ☒ **Revise pages 60, 61, 62** ➤

28 Starting a story

Look at this first sentence from a student's imaginative writing:

> I could hear shouting and screaming. It was getting louder – and closer.

Which of these techniques has this student used to create an engaging opening?
Tick all that apply.

☐ **A** vivid description

☐ **B** dialogue

☐ **C** a mystery

☐ **D** conflict or danger

☑ ☒ **Revise page 63** ➤

29 Planning a transactional text

Which of these statements are **true**?
Tick all that apply.

☐ **A** Information guides, reports, argument and persuasive texts should have an introduction.

☐ **B** Information guides, reports, argument and persuasive texts should have a conclusion.

☐ **C** Information guides, reports, argument and persuasive texts should contain facts.

☐ **D** You do not need to consider your audience when you write an information guide or a report.

☑ ☒ **Revise pages 65, 66** ➤

Knowledge check

30 Beginning a transactional text

Look at this first sentence from a student's transactional writing:

> It is difficult to believe that in the UK the average person produces over 400kg of rubbish every year.

Which one of these techniques has this student used to create an engaging opening?

- [ ] **A** a surprising statistic
- [ ] **B** a rhetorical question
- [ ] **C** an anecdote
- [ ] **D** a controversial statement

☑ ☒ Revise page 67

31 Ending a transactional text

Look at this final sentence from a student's transactional writing:

> If we do not act now, what will we do when it's too late to do anything?

Which one of these techniques has this student used to create an engaging opening?

- [ ] **A** a happy note
- [ ] **B** a warning
- [ ] **C** a thought-provoking rhetorical question
- [ ] **D** a call to action

☑ ☒ Revise page 68

32 Paragraphing

Which of these paragraph structures should you use for which purpose? Draw lines linking them.

Paragraph structure	Writing purpose
point + evidence + explain	narrative
topic sentence + detail/development	argue and persuade
neither of the above	inform, explain, review

☑ ☒ Revise page 70

33 Adverbials

One of the following adverbials could be used to fill the gap in each of the sentences below.

Consequently	For example	However	Moreover

Choose one to fill each gap.

(a) The tigers' habitat is being destroyed.

……………………………….. their numbers have been declining.

(b) Many children will not eat Brussels sprouts.

……………………………….., they will eat peas and carrots.

(c) Exercise is vital for a healthy body.

……………………………….., it is vital for a healthy mind.

(d) Being a celebrity can be stressful.

……………………………….. they are constantly being watched by the press.

☑ ☒ Revise page 71

34 Synonyms

Which of the words below are synonyms? Tick all that apply.

- [ ] **A** hot
- [ ] **B** cold
- [ ] **C** freezing
- [ ] **D** friendly
- [ ] **E** chilly
- [ ] **F** soporific

☑ ☒ Revise page 73

35 Emotive language

> The thought of having to care for a tiny baby is _____ .

Which one of the words below would complete this sentence to give it the greatest emotive emphasis?

☐ **A** appalling   ☐ **B** upsetting

☐ **C** worrying   ☐ **D** terrifying

☐ **E** disturbing   ☐ **F** strange

☑ ☒ **Revise page 74**

36 Using rhetorical devices

Identify the rhetorical devices used in each of the sentences below. Tick all that apply.

(a)
> I felt as though I would be crying for the rest of my life.

☐ **A** rhetorical question

☐ **B** direct address

☐ **C** list

☐ **D** hyperbole

(b)
> Every day, I get up, go to school, come home, do my homework and go to bed.

☐ **A** rhetorical question

☐ **B** direct address

☐ **C** list

☐ **D** hyperbole

(c)
> How many times must we hear this?

☐ **A** rhetorical question

☐ **B** direct address

☐ **C** list

☐ **D** hyperbole

☑ ☒ **Revise pages 75, 76**

37 Using figurative language

Identify the figurative language features used in each of the sentences below.

(a) > Exams creep up on you on silent feet.

☐ **A** simile

☐ **B** metaphor

☐ **C** personification

(b) > Her thoughts buzzed like wasps trapped in a jam jar.

☐ **A** simile

☐ **B** metaphor

☐ **C** personification

(c) > Life is a circus and we are all clowns.

☐ **A** simile

☐ **B** metaphor

☐ **C** personification

☑ ☒ **Revise page 77**

38 The five senses

Which of the five senses has not been used in this student's description?

> The crackle of flames and the fierce heat on my face told me we were in serious danger. The stench of smoke was overpowering my lungs and the taste of hot ash filled my mouth.

Answer: ....

☑ ☒ **Revise page 78**

39 **First and third person**

Re-write the sentence below in the first person.

| He crashed the car when she told him. |

Answer: ....

....

☑ ☒ **Revise page 79**

40 **Sentence types**

Fill the gap in each of the sentences below using a conjunction to link the two clauses.

(a) It grew dark .... soon I was cold.

(b) I tried to warm myself up by running on the spot

.... it didn't work.

(c) .... I had left in a hurry, I hadn't

thought to bring a coat.

(d) ....I couldn't get myself warm,

I would have to go back home.

☑ ☒ **Revise pages 82, 84**

41 **Sentence starts**

The sentences below all begin with a different word class. Draw lines linking each sentence to the word class of its first word.

Word class

| She stared at me. |
| Through the wall, I could hear voices. |
| Slowly, I edged backwards. |
| Creaking loudly, the door opened. |

| pronoun |
| adverb |
| present participle |
| preposition |

☑ ☒ **Revise page 83**

42 **Sentence punctuation**

Some of the sentences below contain a punctuation mistake. Draw lines linking each sentence to the correct comment.

| Animals are mistreated all over the world, this is a disgrace. |
| Although it is clearly wrong, nothing is done to stop it. |
| Why can this not be stopped. |

| should end with a question mark |
| the comma should be a full stop |
| contains no errors |

☑ ☒ **Revise page 86**

43 Using commas

Some of the sentences below are missing a comma. Which ones? Tick all that apply.

☐ **A** I cried when I first went to school.

☐ **B** When I first went to school I cried.

☐ **C** My friend who I had known from nursery could not understand what was wrong.

☐ **D** She laughed made new friends played with them all and had a great time.

☑ ☒ **Revise page 87**

44 Apostrophes

Some of the sentences below are missing an apostrophe. Which ones? Tick all that apply.

☐ **A** Some childrens parents collected them.

☐ **B** Most of us had to get on one of the school buses.

☐ **C** Someone asked if I was alright but I couldnt answer.

☐ **D** My mums words echoed in my ears.

☑ ☒ **Revise pages 88, 91, 92**

45 Advanced punctuation

Which of the punctuation marks could fill the box in the sentence below? Tick all that apply.

Exercise is fun ☐ it should be compulsory.

☐ **A** a semi-colon   ☐ **B** a colon

☐ **C** a dash   ☐ **D** brackets

☑ ☒ **Revise page 89**

46 Checking for common errors

Which of the words below are spelt incorrectly? Tick all that apply.

☐ **A** suddenley   ☐ **B** lately

☐ **C** argument   ☐ **D** dissapointing

☐ **E** beginning   ☐ **F** beleive

☐ **G** dicision   ☐ **H** rhythm

☑ ☒ **Revise pages 91, 93, 94**

Answers to the Knowledge check are on pages 18 and 19 of this booklet.

My catch-up plan

Use this page to make your own customised catch-up plan. Write down all the pages that you plan to revise, then use the tick boxes to track your progress.

Page	Had a go	Nearly there	Nailed it!
......	☐	☐	☐
......	☐	☐	☐
......	☐	☐	☐
......	☐	☐	☐
......	☐	☐	☐
......	☐	☐	☐
......	☐	☐	☐
......	☐	☐	☐
......	☐	☐	☐
......	☐	☐	☐
......	☐	☐	☐
......	☐	☐	☐
......	☐	☐	☐
......	☐	☐	☐
......	☐	☐	☐
......	☐	☐	☐
......	☐	☐	☐
......	☐	☐	☐
......	☐	☐	☐
......	☐	☐	☐
......	☐	☐	☐
......	☐	☐	☐
......	☐	☐	☐
......	☐	☐	☐

Page	Had a go	Nearly there	Nailed it!
......	☐	☐	☐
......	☐	☐	☐
......	☐	☐	☐
......	☐	☐	☐
......	☐	☐	☐
......	☐	☐	☐
......	☐	☐	☐
......	☐	☐	☐
......	☐	☐	☐
......	☐	☐	☐
......	☐	☐	☐
......	☐	☐	☐
......	☐	☐	☐
......	☐	☐	☐
......	☐	☐	☐
......	☐	☐	☐
......	☐	☐	☐
......	☐	☐	☐
......	☐	☐	☐
......	☐	☐	☐
......	☐	☐	☐
......	☐	☐	☐
......	☐	☐	☐
......	☐	☐	☐

Use this page to make any other catch-up notes you need. You could list topics that you know you need extra help with, or make a note of any facts or definitions you are struggling to remember. Or you could use it to record dates and times of catch-up sessions, extra tutorials or study periods.

Matching chart

You can use this chart to help you choose pages for your catch-up plan. Tick the topics and skills you want to revise, and then add the pages listed to your plan on page 14.

Reading skills / topics	Paper	Revision Guide / Workbook pages	Revise? ☑
Reading and understanding	1, 2		☐
Skimming and annotating	1, 2	6, 7	☐
Identifying key information	1, 2	10	☐
Inference	1, 2	11, 12, 13	☐
Commenting on the writer's choices	1, 2		☐
Supporting ideas with evidence	1, 2	14, 15	☐
Commenting on language choice in fiction texts	1	18, 19, 20, 21, 22, 23, 25, 26	☐
Commenting on language choice in non-fiction texts	2	18, 19, 20, 25, 26	☐
Commenting on the writer's use of evidence and opinion	2	27	☐
Commenting on sentence structure	1, 2	28, 29	☐
Commenting on text structure: fiction	1	31	☐
Commenting on text structure: non-fiction	2	30	☐
Comparing texts	2		☐
Synthesis	2	34, 35, 36	☐
Comparing ideas and perspectives	2	34, 37, 38, 39, 40	☐
Evaluating a text	1, 2		☐
Evaluating fiction texts	1	42, 43	☐
Evaluating non-fiction texts	2	42, 44	☐

If you recognise any of these skills or topics from work you did at home during lockdown, add them to your catch-up plan. You can also check with your teacher to find out exactly which topics you should have covered during lockdown.

Writing skills / topics	Paper	Revision Guide / Workbook pages	Revise? ☑
Planning	1, 2		☐
Planning: imaginative writing	1	50	☐
Planning: transactional writing	2	51, 52, 53, 56, 57, 58	☐
Structure	1, 2		☐
Structuring imaginative writing	1	60, 61, 62, 63	☐
Structuring transactional writing	2	65, 66, 67, 68	☐
Paragraphing	1, 2	70, 71	☐
Vocabulary	1, 2		☐
Vocabulary for imaginative writing	1	73, 75, 76, 77, 78, 79	☐
Vocabulary for transactional writing	2	73, 74, 75, 76, 77	☐
Sentences	1, 2		☐
Structuring sentences	1, 2	82, 83, 84	☐
Spelling, punctuation and proofreading	1, 2		☐
Punctuation	1, 2	86, 87, 88, 89	☐
Spelling and proofreading	1, 2	91, 92, 93, 94	☐

You will take two papers for your English Language GCSE. Both papers include reading and writing sections, and many of the skills you have learned in your course will be relevant to both papers. You can use the second column in the matching chart to work out which paper or papers each skill is relevant for.

There is more about the types of questions and texts on each paper on pages 1–5 and pages 47–49 of your Revision Guide.

Knowledge check answers

1

In a **fiction** text you need to think about		purpose
		character
In a **non-fiction** text you need to think about		atmosphere
		tone
		point of view

2 A, B, C and D
3 C
4 B
5 grownups
6 D
7

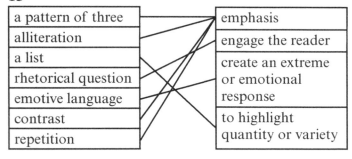

The narrator makes us feel sorry for him. He tells us he was "doubly an orphan because both his parents are dead, and that he had been "reared in a workhouse" and, even though he works hard, he is not respected in his job. I, Samuel Lowgood, who had worked and slaved and drudged, had been snubbed, throughout eleven long weary years".

The first short quotation and the final longer quotations are not enclosed in quotation marks. The final longer quotation should be introduced with a colon.

8 C
9 The words "worked", "slaved" and "drudged" are verbs.
10 A, B and D
11 C
12 A, C and D
13 A, B and C
14 First person
15

a pattern of three		emphasis
alliteration		engage the reader
a list		create an extreme or emotional response
rhetorical question		
emotive language		
contrast		to highlight quantity or variety
repetition		

16 (a) opinion; (b) fact; (c) expert evidence
17 1: The student has incorrectly identified the sentence type: this is a multi-clause sentence.

2: The comment is inaccurate: the writer uses the multi-clause sentence to highlight the number of different reasons why no one wants to do a paper round.

18

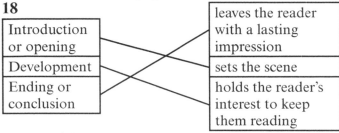

Introduction or opening		leaves the reader with a lasting impression
Development		sets the scene
Ending or conclusion		holds the reader's interest to keep them reading

19 B and D
20 C and D
21 A and D
22 D
23 C
24 B
25 B
26 (a) A letter: your address
(b) A newspaper article: sub-heading
(c) An information guide: sub-heading and bullet points
27 4   falling action
    5   resolution
    2   rising action
    1   exposition
    3   climax
28 C and D
29 A, B and C
30 A
31 C
32

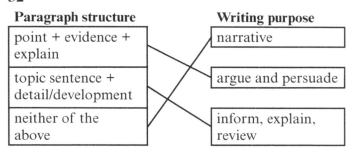

Paragraph structure		**Writing purpose**
point + evidence + explain		narrative
topic sentence + detail/development		argue and persuade
neither of the above		inform, explain, review

33 (a) Consequently
(b) However
(c) Moreover
(d) For example
34 B, C and E
35 D
36 (a) D
(b) C
(c) A and B

37 (a) C personification
   (b) A simile
   (c) B metaphor
38 Sight
39 I crashed the car when she told me. /
   He crashed the car when I told him.
40 (a) and / so
   (b) but / however
   (c) because / as
   (d) if

41

	Word class
She stared at me.	pronoun
Through the wall, I could hear voices.	adverb
Slowly, I edged backwards.	present participle
Creaking loudly, the door opened.	preposition

42

Animals are mistreated all over the world, this is a disgrace.	should end with a question mark
Although it is clearly wrong, nothing is done to stop it.	the comma should be a full stop
Why can this not be stopped.	contains no errors

43 B, C and D
44 A, C and D
45 A and C
46 A, D, F and G

Published by Pearson Education Limited,
80 Strand, London, WC2R 0RL.

www.pearsonschoolsandfecolleges.co.uk

Copies of official specifications for all Pearson qualifications may be found on the website: qualifications.pearson.com

Text and illustrations © Pearson Education Ltd 2020
Produced, typeset and illustrated by Florence Production Ltd, Stoodleigh, Devon, UK

Cover illustration thumbnails by Pearson Education Ltd

The right of David Grant to be identified as author of this work has been asserted by him in accordance with the Copyright, Designs and Patents Act 1988.

First published 2020
23 22 21 20
10 9 8 7 6 5 4 3 2 1

British Library Cataloguing in Publication Data
A catalogue record for this book is available from the British Library

ISBN 9781292374857

Printed in the UK by Ashford Colour Press

Acknowledgements

P5, 18 Extract from Samual Lowgood's Revenge, Mary Elizabeth Braddon (1835–1915); **P5, P7** Extract from 'Who'd be a paper boy?', The Guardian, 11/03/2006 (Crace J) Guardian News and Media Limited; **P6** Extract from 'The Half Brothers', Elizabeth Gaskill (1810–1865); **P6** Extract from Angela's Ashes, HarperCollins Publishers Ltd © Frank McCourt, 2005; **P7** Extract from 'The history of London's black cabs', The Guardian, 09/12/2012 (Beetlestone I) Guardian News and Media Limited

Notes from the publisher

1. While the publishers have made every attempt to ensure that advice on the qualification and its assessment is accurate, the official specification and associated assessment guidance materials are the only authoritative source of information and should always be referred to for definitive guidance.

Pearson examiners have not contributed to any sections in this resource relevant to examination papers for which they have responsibility.

2. Pearson has robust editorial processes, including answer and fact checks, to ensure the accuracy of the content in this publication, and every effort is made to ensure this publication is free of errors. We are, however, only human, and occasionally errors do occur. Pearson is not liable for any misunderstandings that arise as a result of errors in this publication, but it is our priority to ensure that the content is accurate. If you spot an error, please do contact us at resourcescorrections@pearson.com so we can make sure it is corrected.

ISBN 978-1-292-37485-7